# Forelocks, Fetlocks, & Horse Tales



Rocking Horse Press

# Forelocks, Fetlocks, & Horse Tales

Written by Kim Marie Wood

Cover photo by Debbie Uecker-Keough
338 N. Cuyamaca St.
El Cajon, CA 92020
www.photobydebbie.com

Rocking Horse Press

Rocking Horse Press
P.O. Box 21
Oshtemo, Michigan 49077-0021
(269) 345-3783

Visit us online at www.rockinghorsepress.com



Library of Congress Cataloging-in-Publication Date
Wood, Kim Marie
Forelocks, Fetlocks & Horse Tales / Kim Marie Wood
p. cm.
ISBN 0-9671978-6-4 (pbk.)
1. Fiction-Children's Horse Stories
I. Wood, Kim Marie
II. Title

99-68039
CIP

Second Edition
1 2 3 4 5 6 7 8 9 0
Printed in the United States of America

ISBN 0-9671978-6-4 5.95

Dedicated to Mingo and Tsabre, our first and very special horses.

# Ask Henry

Mallory struggled with the wheelbarrow. "I've filled it too full again, Ginger," she said aloud to the horse in the stall next to her. "When am I going to learn to make more trips, instead of trying to push this heavy thing out of the barn?"

This Saturday morning Mallory had already mucked six stalls before the first boarder arrived.

"Oh, goody," exclaimed Karen, a twelve year old redhead with a face full of freckles. "I'm so glad Ginger hasn't gone out yet. That saves me having to go out to the pasture and catch her up."

"I was going to let her out as soon as I empty this. You got here just in time," Mallory told her.

"For once, I think Ginger and I will be tacked up, warmed up and ready for our lesson on time," said the freckle-faced girl happily. "Connie won't believe it!"

Just then, Connie came in the barn. "What won't I believe?" Connie was Oak Haven Farm's resident trainer and riding instructor.

"I'm your 10:00 lesson," answered Karen. "And it's only 9:30 now. We'll be ready on time."

"Not unless you stop talking and get moving," said Connie good-naturedly. "How are things going with you, Mallory?"

"I'll have the stalls done by noon, Connie. Do you have time for my lesson after lunch?"

"Of course. You work so hard to earn your lesson, I'll make the time. How about 1:00?"

Thinking about her lesson made it easier for Mallory to get back to her chores. While she didn't have her own horse, she enjoyed riding the school horses at Oak Haven. Her deal with Connie traded three hours of barn chores for a one-hour lesson.

With her chores done, Mallory decided to eat her lunch on the barn's front porch swing. She looked up to see a dark blue truck pulling a matching four-horse trailer making its way up the long driveway. "Wow," she thought to herself. "What a fancy rig." The driver climbed out of the cab and approached Mallory. "I'm supposed to deliver this horse to Oak Haven Farm. I left last night and I've been on the road for thirteen hours. I gave this guy some water and hay, but someone's going to have to get him out of the trailer for me."

"Let me go find Connie. I'll be right back," promised Mallroy. She found Connie in the indoor arena, just finishing a lesson. "Connie," she called. "Someone is here to deliver a horse. What should I do?"

Connie looked concerned. "We don't have any horses scheduled to arrive. I'd better go with you and see what's up."

By the time they got out front, it was too late. A tall bay horse was standing by the paddock gate, head hanging low. A long bloody gash ran down one side of his face. The truck driver stood helplessly behind the open trailer door, holding a broken halter in his hands.

"He was hollering and stomping to get out, so I opened the back door. But I guess he'd already broken his halter. He ran out with his head up and banged it on the trailer door."

"He did more than bang it," cried Connie with horror. "He's got a really ugly laceration. Mallory, run inside and call Dr. Kingston. Tell him we have an emergency. I'll try and get him into the paddock. And bring a halter and lead rope back with you!"

Mallory found Dr. Kingston's emergency pager number next to the phone. She dialed it and left a breathless call for help. Within two minutes, Dr. Kingston called back to say he was on his way. Mallory grabbed a halter and lead rope off the wall and ran back to Connie.

Connie had managed to get the unhappy horse into the small front paddock, but was having no luck getting close to him. Every time she took a step toward him, he would back away three steps. "All right, fella. We'll wait for Dr. Kingston to get here. In the meantime, I need to figure out who you are."

The poor truck driver looked almost as miserable as the horse. "It was an accident, ma'am. I've hauled lots of horses, but I've never had anything like this happen before. Is the horse going to be okay?"

"He's going to need stitches or staples for sure," said Connie. "The vet will be here soon. But I don't know this horse and I don't have authorization to have him treated."

Mallory was listening to the conversation, but she couldn't take her eyes off the injured horse.

"I've got papers for him in my truck. Someone here is supposed to sign for him."

The truck driver produced a manila envelope from the truck seat. Connie found the horse's registration papers. "Well, now he's got a name. The papers say he's Ask Henry. Six-year-old Thoroughbred, owned by Karl Matthews. But why is he here? I'm not expecting any horses this month."

Mallory perked up at the mention of the horse's name. "Okay Henry," she said softly. "It's going to be okay, big guy." Henry lifted his head slightly at the sound of his name, but then it dropped again.

"Mr. Matthews lives in Kentucky, but he has a vacation home near here," explained the truck driver. "He said he visited your farm last summer. You mean, you never got the message that this horse was coming?"

"That's exactly what I'm saying," said Connie. "I'm not sure what to do, but this horse has to be taken care of right now."

"Isn't there a signed boarding contract with those papers?" asked the truck driver. "And the check for the first two months board?"

Connie looked through the rest of the papers in the envelope. "You're right," she said. "He must have picked these up when he visited. But we don't have a stall for him until next month. This is going to be tricky. At least, now we have permission for Dr. Kingston to do his job."

"If you can sign this receiving slip, I need to get going. I want to check into a hotel and get some sleep before driving back," said the truck driver.

Connie looked confused. "You HAVE to take him, Connie," pleaded Mallory. "He's in trouble. He needs our help. Can't we find his owner later?"

With that, the truck driver climbed back in the cab and started the engine. Connie shook her head as the truck and trailer drove away. A few minutes later, Dr. Kingston's familiar green station wagon appeared.

Mallory had forgotten about her lesson. She couldn't take her eyes off Henry. She was still holding the halter and lead rope, waiting for the vet to tell them what to do.

"We don't know anything about this horse, but there are no allergies listed," Connie was quick to say. Dr. Kingston eyed the situation.

"His name is Henry," said Mallory. At the sound of his name, Henry tried to lift his head, but it was too much effort.

"Let me see if I can get a halter on him," said Connie. Fortunately, Henry stood quietly as Connie buckled the halter and snapped on the lead rope.

"He seems pretty quiet. We need to be careful about shock, though. Let's try and take care of him out here," instructed Dr. Kingston. After examining the wound and checking the horse's vital signs, he gave Henry a mild tranquilizer to help him relax. After a few minutes, Henry's breathing slowed and became more regular.

"This is going to be a little tricky," said the vet. "I think I'll need to use staples for this laceration. Facial lacerations aren't always simple to close."

Connie held Henry's lead rope while Mallory helped Dr. Kingston get the things he needed from the back of his station wagon.

"Mallory, I'll need your help, too," said Dr. Kingston. "Do you think you can hold the lead rope and just talk quietly to him while we fix him up?"

Dr. Kingston worked patiently for more than an hour. Connie assisted the vet while Mallory stroked Henry's neck. "It's going to be okay, Henry," repeated Mallory softly.

When Dr. Kingston was done, Henry had seventeen staples closing the wound. "We need to give him a tetanus shot, then we can put him in a stall."

"We don't have any stalls available in the big barn," said Connie.

"But the big stall in the foaling shed is empty," offered Mallory.

Connie sighed. "I'm glad YOU'RE thinking, Mallory! Why don't you get it set up for him with bedding, hay and water?"

Mallory handed the lead rope to Connie and walked into the barn. Once inside, she ran out the back door to inspect the foaling shed. In ten minutes she had it all set up for Henry.

Connie handed Mallory the lead rope. "See if he'll go with you, Mallory. I'll take care of the rest of the details with Dr. Kingston."

"Come on, Henry," Mallory urged the bay gelding. "We've got a special place just for you." Henry hesitated, then slowly walked off with Mallory. He started and stopped several times along the way, but finally Mallory had him bedded down inside the foaling shed. After a couple of minutes, Henry groaned and lay down. His legs were tucked under himself like a little foal. Mallory hurried back to find Connie and Dr. Kingston.

"He's got good gut sounds and his temperature is pretty normal. I don't think it's colic," reported Dr. Kingston. "But you're going to need to keep a close eye on him, and call me if anything changes. I'll stop back later in the week and check on him if I don't hear from you."

"I'll sit with him," volunteered Mallory. "My chores are done and I've got a book to read."

"Well, then I could get busy on the phone tracking down Mr. Matthews. That would be a big help, Mallory," said Connie.

Mallory spent the rest of the afternoon sitting in the corner of the big stall, reading her book and watching Henry's every move. After a little while, his nose rested on the ground and he seemed to be taking a nap. Mallory checked her watch so she would know how long he had been down.

After a half an hour, Henry groaned loudly and struggled to stand. It took him a couple of tries, but finally he was up. He walked on shaky legs over to the manger. He sniffed the hay, but ignored it. The water bucket seemed to catch his interest. He took a long, slow drink and groaned again. Mallory got up and approached him, talking softly. "Easy, Henry. Good boy. Does that water taste good?"

Henry slowly turned toward Mallory, showing the long gash on his face. Mallory gasped. "Oh, you poor thing. What a horrible first day. And no one here you even know."

"He seems to know you," said Connie. She had arrived with Henry's pain medication. "See if he'll take this from you, Mallory. I've crushed the tablets and mixed them with a little grain and applesauce."

Connie waited at the stall door and Mallory coaxed Henry to take the medicated treat. "You're doing a wonderful job with him, Mallory. I called your folks to let them know you were still here. Your mom said you could stay awhile longer, if you want."

Awhile longer turned into a few more hours. Mallory looked up to see her dad standing at Henry's stall door. "Your mom sent me with supper for you. Connie was pretty sure we wouldn't get you to come home."

"Thanks, Dad! His name is Henry and he doesn't have a person of his own. I was so worried about whether he was going to eat, I forgot about my own stomach."

"Connie's at her house across the street. She wants you to call her from the barn phone if you need anything. Mom will come back and pick you up at bedtime. I brought you a blanket and a flashlight. It's going to get dark soon."

Henry stayed up, but moved little. When her mom arrived, Mallory had lost track of time.

"You can call Connie before we leave," said her mom. "It's late, almost eleven."

From inside the barn, Mallory dialed the house. "He's been quiet all evening, Connie. And his temperature is normal, 99 degrees." Mallory's mom rushed in. "He's upset about something," she said. "Come quick!"

"Gotta go!" Mallory said as she slammed down the receiver.

Henry was banging on the stall door with a front foot and shaking his head. His whinny sounded sad. "It's okay, Henry. It's okay," soothed Mallory. At the sound of Mallory's voice, Henry quieted. Connie rushed across the street to see what was happening. "He doesn't want to be alone," Mallory explained. "He got upset when I left."

Henry reached across the stall door and rested his head lightly on Mallory's shoulder. "I think he wants YOU to stay," said Connie.

"Can I, Mom? Is it okay?" Mallory asked hopefully.

"As long as you don't actually sleep IN the stall, I guess it would be okay," said her mom.

Connie returned from the barn with a pillow and sleeping bag. "You never know, so I keep these in my office," she explained.

Mallory made up her bed in front of Henry's stall door. He seemed satisfied that she wasn't going to leave again, and took a few nibbles of hay. "That's a good sign," observed Connie.

"I think Henry will be feeling a little better by tomorrow. I reached Mr. Matthews by phone. He feels awful and said he'd be here by suppertime tomorrow."

Mallory woke up every hour or so to check on Henry. Each time she found him standing near the stall door, dozing quietly. She was satisfied.

Connie showed up early in the morning with orange juice and a bagel for Mallory. She looked pleased. "I think the worst is over, Mallory. Henry's eyes look brighter and he even looks interested in your bagel."

Mallory broke off a piece of bagel and offered it to him. He sniffed it then gobbled it up. Mallory grinned.

"Now I want you to go home, young lady. Take a bath and take a nap. I don't want to see you back here until after lunch!"

Waking up in her own bed, Mallory looked at the clock on her dresser. It was almost 2:00. She quickly got dressed and looked for her parents. She found her dad in the garage. "I suppose you want to go back and see that horse?" asked her father.

"Please, Dad. He really likes me. May I?"

"Mom's at the store. She said it would be all right, as long as you ate something before you left."

"Deal," exclaimed Mallory, running into the kitchen. She made a sandwich and grabbed an apple and a juice box. "Take an apple for yourself, too," scolded her dad, knowingly.

Mallory jumped on her bike and sped to Oak Haven. Henry nickered as she approached the foaling shed.

"Yes, I'm back," she told him. "How about an apple?"

Henry eagerly took the offered apple. Again, he rested his head softly on Mallory's shoulder. Mallory closed her eyes and enjoyed the quiet moment.

"You've got a friend," said an unfamiliar man's voice. "Henry doesn't like just anyone."

Mallory turned around to find a tall man about her dad's age.

"I'm Kurt Matthews. You must be Mallory. I've heard all about what a great job you did helping Henry. I owe you a lot."

"I just love horses. He needed me yesterday. I'm sure he's glad to see you," said Mallory, backing away a few steps.

"Henry is the last horse out of my favorite mare. I travel a lot and don't have much time to ride, but I can't part with him. I thought I might be able to ride some in the summer if I brought him here," explained Mr. Matthews.

"Oak Haven is great," said Mallory. "I've been taking lessons from Connie for three years."

"I know," he answered. "Connie spent the last hour telling me all about you. Especially how hard you work and how well you ride. Would you be interested in taking care of Henry for me?"

"Sure," Mallory answered quickly. "I'd be happy to add him to my chores!"

"That wasn't what I had in mind. I mean, if it's okay with your parents, I'd like you to ride him for me and take care of him. Just like he was your horse. Then, when I visit, I can take him for a ride. I know he'd be happy and I wouldn't have to worry about him. He's going to spend this summer healing up his face, but next summer maybe you could show him?" Mallory couldn't answer right away. Henry turned to look at her. "His registered name is 'Ask Henry.' What do you think, fella? Do you want Mallory to be your special friend?" Henry nickered his vote of approval.

Mr. Matthews shook Mallory's hand and asked, "How about introducing me to your parents?"

# Squirt

"It's time! It's time!" shouted a voice on the other end of the phone. Liz knew immediately that it was Amanda at the other end. That could mean only one thing: Sierra was foaling!

"I'm on my way! Bye!" said Liz as she slammed down the phone. As she hurried to put on her boots, she called to her mother upstairs, "It's time, Mom! I gotta go!"

"Don't forget to wear your bike helmet, Liz!" came her mother's voice. Liz was already buckling her helmet as she ran to the garage for her bike. It was only a ten minute ride to Windy Wood Farm, but Liz was going to set a new record today.

Her best friend Amanda was pacing back and forth on the front porch, waiting for her as she rode up the long driveway. "I can't believe it's finally happening," exclaimed Amanda. And we still haven't thought of a name! Mom said we can go in the barn if we're quiet. Sierra is in the big box stall on the end."

The two girls entered the barn as quietly as they could. Amanda's father was carrying a fresh bucket of water to Sierra's stall. "This isn't going to happen right away," he said. "This may take a few hours. Go ahead and take a look in the stall, so you can both see that Sierra's fine. I'll come and get you when things start to happen."

Liz and Amanda peeked over the stall door. The big buckskin mare was standing in the corner, head down, breathing deeply but calmly.

"Hi, Sierra," Liz said. Sierra nickered quietly in response to her name.

"You girls need something to do," said Amanda's father with a smile. "This would be a perfect time for you two to clean up the tack room. Spring cleaning, you know."

The girls spent the next few hours cleaning and organizing the tack room. They even swept the cobwebs from the ceiling. When that was done, they went back to look into Sierra's stall. She was laying on her side now, breathing heavier. She lifted her head up to look at the girls, and then laid it back down on the straw. Amanda's father came up behind them.

"It won't be long now. By the time you wash all the brushes and scrub out those water buckets, the baby should be on it's way."
The girls looked at each other and smiled.
A lot of chores were sure getting done today!

Behind the barn, Liz and Amanda were finishing rinsing out the last bucket. "Okay, ladies, enough chores. It's time!" called Amanda's father. They turned off the hose and ran to the barn door. Once inside, they walked slowly and quietly to Sierra's stall. Amanda's mother was standing near the stall door. She motioned for the girls to come closer. First to emerge were tiny hooves, followed by thin little legs. A nose appeared next, as the girls watched in amazement. In less than thirty minutes there was a newborn foal lying on the straw next to his mother. Standing over him, Sierra licked him gently and nuzzled him whenever he moved.

"He's a gruella, just like his daddy," announced Amanda's father. "Look at the beautiful dorsal stripe running down the middle of his back. And when he's completely dried off, I'll bet we'll see zebra stripes on his legs, too." The foal chose that moment to try and stand up. It took several attempts, but Sierra nuzzled him encouragingly until he was successful. In less than five minutes, he was nursing happily.

"We still don't have a name," Amanda reminded everyone.

"I'll put you girls in charge of that one," answered her father. "Spend some time watching him for the next few days, and the right name will come along." Liz spent the night at Amanda's house, so they could check on the new foal every few hours. After breakfast the next morning, Amanda's father put Sierra and the new colt into the grassy green paddock next to the barn. The girls stood at the fence and watched as Sierra grazed on the fresh grass. The gruella colt trotted around on his wobbly legs, staying near his mother. His black mane and tail were a contrast to his mousy brown coat. His tiny ears were also black-tipped. High on each leg were four dark leg bars, like stripes on a zebra. His dorsal stripe looked as if someone had taken a magic marker and drawn a line from the bottom of his mane all the way to his tail.

"Time for church," announced Amanda's mother. "They'll still be here when we get back." The girls reluctantly got into the back seat, wishing they could stay home with the horses. After church, Amanda's parents wanted to have lunch in town, but the girls would have no part of it. They would go without lunch if it got them home faster!

As they pulled into the driveway, it was clear something was wrong! Inside the paddock, Sierra was pacing madly along the fence, whinnying loudly. Outside the fence was the gruella colt, trying to get back to his mother.

"How on earth did that happen?" wondered Amanda's father aloud. "The gate is still locked and that is a three-board fence." He got a lead rope from the barn and put it on Sierra. Amanda held the gate open as the colt scrambled back inside. As soon as Sierra was sure he way okay, she let him nurse.

The girls ate their lunches outside, refusing to take their eyes off the mother and baby. "First we have to figure out how he got out," said Liz.

"Then we have to come up with a name," added Amanda. They kept watch all afternoon, but everything seemed peaceful.

Sierra chose to take a break beneath the shade of the big oak tree next to the fence, her favorite resting spot. After a little while, the colt laid down for a nap next to his mother. He lay flat on his side, sleeping quietly between his mother and the paddock fence. Amanda ran back to the house to get her camera. They had been so excited, they had forgotten to take any pictures!

As Amanda came back from the house, it happened. As the colt started to wake up, he rolled over on his other side AND under the bottom board of the fence! Once again, he was on one side and his mother was on the other. "Dad," yelled Amanda, "Come quickly! Hurry up!"

"What's the matter? What's going on?" asked Amanda's father.

"The colt has gotten out again, that's what!"

He laid down to take a nap. When he started to wake up he rolled over and just squirted right under the fence," exclaimed Amanda.

"That's it," said Liz. "That's his name. Squirt!"

"Perfect," agreed Amanda.

"Fine with me," added Amanda's father. "But let's hope he outgrows this soon!"

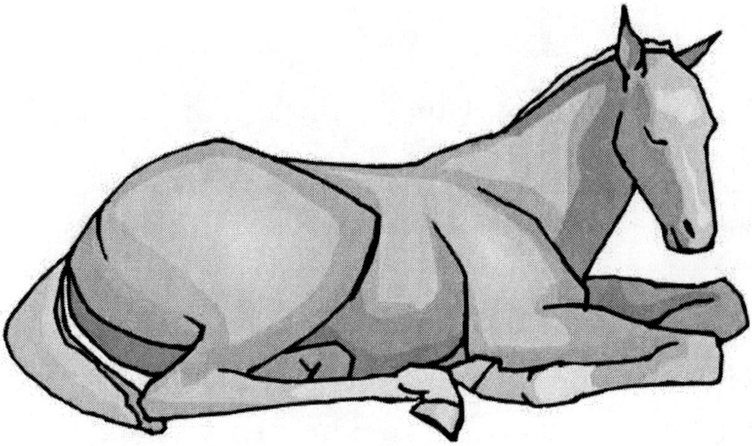

## On the Farm

"Just great!" complained Anna. "Not only do we have to move away from all our friends, but we have to live with Grandma and Grandpa for the rest of the summer!"

"Mom and Dad already told you, they have to sell the house. Besides, you always liked staying here on the farm," offered her ten-year-old brother. "What's the big deal?"

"Look James, you KNOW I love Grandma and Grandpa. But visiting for two weeks in the summer is different from leaving the city permanently. We're moving to the middle of nowhere for good! No more walking a few blocks to do practically anything you want to do. And most of our neighbors here will have either fur or feathers!" Sitting on the picnic table in their grandparents' backyard, the idea of moving had really sunk in. For James, his sense of adventure helped him see that moving could be "way cool." But for Anna, at twelve, it seemed like a jail sentence, leaving both her friends and familiar life behind. A honking horn made them both turn around. It was their family car pulling up the long gravel driveway. James ran to greet his parents, but Anna lagged behind, refusing to just go along with everything so easily.

"Help us carry in these groceries, you two!" called their father. "Your mother bought out the store, trying to stock Grandma and Grandpa with all your favorites!"

"Alright, Mom! You got my favorite cereal!" James grinned.

"You'll find lots of your favorite things inside those bags, once you carry them into the house," said their mother. "Come on Anna, give us a hand here."

Walking slowly to the car, Anna looked at the number of bags in both the back seat and the trunk. "That's a lot of food, Mom. You are coming back eventually, aren't you?" she asked suspiciously.

Their parents looked at each other and exchanged silent glances of understanding. Anna was going

to be a hard sell. "Come on guys, let's get these groceries put away for Grandma. She'll be busy full-time just trying to feed you both," said their father.

Grandpa met them all at the back door. "Right inside here," he smiled. "As soon as you get the groceries put away, Grandma has lunch ready for us."

Sitting at the long kitchen table, everyone was busy eating lunch and chatting except Anna. She sort of pushed her potato salad around on her plate, picking up her sandwich and putting it down without taking a bite. Careful not to be too obvious as she sulked, Anna asked to be excused to check the mailbox. The driveway was long enough to give her some time to herself if she walked slowly.

It was too soon to expect any mail from her friends, but Anna was still hopeful as she opened the big country mailbox. Although there was nothing with her name on it, she was interested in a postcard for Grandpa that advertised a farmer's auction on Saturday. It listed livestock for sale, as well as farm equipment. It wouldn't be the same as riding a school horse at Meadowbrooke Stable, but maybe there will be some horses there. She decided to ask Grandpa if he was going.

"Well, sure," Grandpa answered. "I always enjoy spending a Saturday at the auction. But Grandma might have something to say about it. I never seem to come home without buying something."

Early Saturday morning, Anna's parents headed back to the city. Hugging both kids, their mother said: "We'll be back in three weeks. Make sure you help out around here and keep your own things picked up. By that time, our new house will be almost done and we'll be moving in right across the street from Grandma and Grandpa."

Everyone waved as their car drove away. "I've packed your lunch. Better get these two kids in the truck and head for the auction, Grandpa."

James didn't need to be asked twice. He was already buckled as Anna climbed in beside him. Grandma waved as they started on their way, hoping Anna would find something to interest her at the auction.

Neither Anna nor James were prepared for the crowd of people and livestock, not to mention all the curious pieces of farm equipment. They could only guess what some of the strange machines were used for. "I'm going to look for a new tiller for the red tractor," said Grandpa. "Do you want to come with me, or would you like to walk through the horse barn over there?"

"Can we really go look at the horses, Grandpa?" asked Anna. It was the first excited expression Grandpa had seen since she arrived a week ago.

"Sure. As long as you two stay together, you can meet me right here in about twenty minutes. Agreed?"

"Okay Grandpa," promised Anna. James had to run a few steps to catch up with her. Inside the horse barn, the narrow walkway was noisy and crowded with people young and old. Traffic would come to a halt as someone stopped to look inside a stall. None of these horses looked like the tall, elegant school horses Anna had ridden at Meadowbrooke. There were a lot of shaggy ponies and horses of all shapes and sizes.

James stopped in front of a pen holding a fat pony. The pony was gray with black spots on her rump. The sign on the stall door said her name was Kachina, and that she was twelve years old. It also advertised that she was broke to ride and pull a cart.

"I like this one best," said James. "She has a friendly face."

Anna rolled her eyes. "That's just a big pony. I ride real horses. And I'm sure we won't find any of those here today." After viewing the rest of the horses, Anna and James went to meet Grandpa. He hadn't found what he was looking for, but Grandpa was still in a good mood.

"How about you two? Anything interesting in the horse barn?"

"We saw a lot of horses, Grandpa. But I don't think we want to stay for the horse auction. It would be too sad," said Anna. Before they left, James insisted on showing Grandpa the fat spotted pony.

"You have a pretty good eye for horse-flesh,

young man. That does look like a fine pony. I used to keep ponies when your father was young, but now I only have cattle. Maybe you'll end up with a pony of your own." As they climbed in the truck to head home, Grandpa saw someone he knew. "I'll be right back." Anna and James waited in the truck. After about ten minutes, Grandpa returned. "James, I need some help fixing a fence. Can you give me a hand when we get home?"

"Sure, Grandpa," James answered eagerly. "I'm a great helper! Just ask my dad."

Soon they pulled into the driveway. Grandma was outside feeding the geese. She carefully examined the back of the truck. "So you came home without buying anything? I can't believe it."

"Well," explained Grandpa. "I've got some fence I want to fix up behind the barn and I wanted to get started. James has even agreed to help."

Sitting at the picnic table, Anna spent her afternoon trying to write letters to her friends, but decided none of them were good enough to send. She looked up as an old truck drove up the driveway, pulling a trailer. Before she could get up and check it out, Grandma was hurrying out the door. “I knew it!” she exclaimed. “I just knew it!”

“What, Grandma? What did you know?” asked Anna, hurrying to catch up with Grandma.

“I knew he couldn’t go to the auction without buying something!”

“But Grandma,” explained Anna, “we didn’t stay for the sale. We came home before it started.”

“Doesn’t mean anything,” laughed Grandma. “He’s played this trick on me before. I’m sure there is something inside that trailer that now belongs here.”

Grandpa was hurrying from behind the barn, with James following close behind. “He was smiling, but not at Grandma. “Karl, you’re early. I wasn’t expecting you until after supper,” he said to the man in the truck. “I’m not quite ready.”

“Well,” said Karl, “I need to get home to feed my critters, so here’s yours!”

Inside the trailer was the gray spotted pony. Grandpa opened the trailer door and waited for Kachina to back out. He took the lead rope from the back of the trailer and snapped it on her halter. “Her paddock isn’t quite ready yet. Anna, I’m going to ask you to hold onto her here in the front yard while James and I finish up.”

James didn't know who to hug, Grandpa or the pony. But he followed Grandpa back to fence mending, excited to know why they had been working so hard all afternoon.

"Are you okay with the pony?" Grandma asked Anna. "Oh, yes, Grandma. I took riding lessons at Meadowbrooke Stable with real horses. I'm sure I can handle this pony."

Kachina was happy to eat grass for the next hour. "No wonder you're so fat," said Anna. You hardly stop to catch a breath." Anna felt a rumble in her stomach. She had gotten so interested in the little pony, she forgot it was past suppertime for herself.

James came to fetch Anna and Kachina. "We're all ready for her now, Anna. Grandpa said to bring her to the side barn door, so we can put her in her stall." The stall was knee-deep in straw and James had already filled a water bucket for her. Soon Kachina was happily munching hay.

"She likes it here, Grandpa," James announced. "Who does she belong to?"

"Well, you picked her out. Will you mind sharing her with Anna?" asked Grandpa.

Anna was quick to answer. "I know all about

horses, Grandpa. I'll teach James how to do chores and take care of her."

"That would at least be something a little fun to do," Anna thought to herself.

For the next week, Anna and James spent nearly every waking minute in or around the barn. Sometimes they just stood by the fence and watched her. "She sure is fat," Anna repeated for the 100th time. "But she seems happy, James. I'm sure she'll lose weight when you start riding her and she gets more exercise."

Early Monday morning Anna and James finished breakfast and went to feed Kachina. Instead of greeting them as they came in the barn, Kachina was standing in the far corner of her stall. Her head was hanging down and she looked tired. James ran back to the house to get Grandpa. "I think Kachina's sick, Grandpa. Come quick."

Grandpa followed James into the barn where Anna waited nervously. "She hasn't touched her hay since last night, Grandpa. Is she sick?"

As Grandpa entered the stall, Kachina backed farther into the corner. He opened her paddock door and sunlight filled the stall. Kachina walked slowly toward the door, then stopped. She turned around and nickered softly.

From out of the corner stepped a tiny black foal with a small white blanket on its rump. The white blanket was speckled with black spots, just like his mother.

Anna and James were hypnotized. "Two for the price of one, Anna," said Grandpa with a knowing smile. "Hope you know something about foals."

Anna was silent but smiling. Okay, Anna decided. There are going to be some pluses to living in the country.

# Christmas Wishes

"It's not fair," complained eleven-year-old Julie. "Why can't my parents be here for Christmas?"

"Denver is snowed in," explained Aunt Jeanne. "The storm closed the airport. They won't be able to fly out until day after tomorrow. They'll just go back and stay with Grandma and Grandpa until then."

Julie's folks had flown to Colorado for what was supposed to be a short visit. Julie stayed with Aunt Jeanne, her father's sister, who lived nearby. Her parents didn't want her to miss any school before vacation.

"Mer-ry Christmas," Julie said, rather unconvincingly. "It's not going to be the same without them here."

"That's true," Aunt Jeanne agreed. "But what an unexpected Christmas present for Grandma and Grandpa. We'll call them tomorrow morning after you and I open our presents."

"Shouldn't we wait until they get home and open presents then?" asked Julie.

"I think we should open ours," answered Aunt Jeanne. "Then, when we talk with them on the phone, we can tell them how much we like our presents."

After Julie and Aunt Jeanne returned home from the Christmas Eve church service, Julie looked closely at the presents under the tree. She saw four packages with her name on them.

"I hope I get some horse stuff," Julie thought to herself. "It would be really nice to have my own set of brushes and things when I go for my lessons, even if I don't have my own horse." None of the packages gave any hint of what was inside.

Aunt Jeanne was sitting in her favorite chair, crocheting and watching the evening news, when Julie came to say good night. Aunt Jeanne was smiling and seemed to be filled with Christmas joy. On her way to bed, Julie decided to try hard to make the best of the situation. As she drifted off to sleep, she reminded herself to wake up happy and not spoil Christmas Day for Aunt Jeanne.

It was still dark outside, but Julie could see a hint of the sun starting to rise. It was odd, waking up in Aunt Jeanne's guest room on Christmas morning. It reminded her that her folks weren't going to be home for Christmas. She allowed herself a moment of self-pity, then greeted Jacob, Aunt Jeanne's big yellow cat. "Let's go wake up Aunt Jeanne and wish her a Merry Christmas," she told the cat.

Julie walked down the hall to Aunt Jeanne's bedroom. Jacob padded behind, too dignified to hurry. Aunt Jeanne's bed wasn't made, but she wasn't in it. When Jacob realized that Julie was heading for the kitchen next, he followed her more quickly, losing a bit of his aloof posture. But Aunt Jeanne wasn't in the kitchen either, although the coffeepot was on. Julie was confused.

Just then, Julie heard the back door open. Aunt Jeanne stomped the snow off her boots and came into the kitchen.

"You sure are up early! I went out to see if the paper was here yet, so I could read it with my morning coffee. Do you want breakfast, or do you want to open presents?"

"We can have breakfast first," suggested Julie. "Grandma and Grandpa and my folks won't be up for awhile, especially since I'm not there to wake them up. Then we can open presents after we eat."

After they finished breakfast, Aunt Jeanne put a CD on with Christmas music. "Now it really feels like Christmas around here," Aunt Jeanne announced. Aunt Jeanne always came to Julie's house for Christmas morning. This would be the first time Julie was somewhere besides home for Christmas.

Aunt Jeanne sat on the floor next to Julie. Jacob immediately joined them near the tree. "Where's Jacob's present?" Julie asked.

"He has some treats in his stocking," said Aunt Jeanne. "But what he's waiting for is for us to unwrap our gifts so he can play with the paper and sit in the boxes. Here, this one's from Grandma and Grandpa for you." Julie carefully opened the package. "It's a winter riding outfit!" Julie exclaimed. "Look, the sweatshirt and tights match!"

"You don't mind getting clothes?" asked Aunt Jeanne.

"Not when they're riding clothes!" Maybe this won't be so hard, Julie thought to herself.

Aunt Jeanne opened her gift from Julie's grandparents in Colorado. "Clothes for me, too!" It was a beautiful navy blue sweater with white snowflakes. "Grandma sure knows me. I love sweaters!" The next package Julie opened was from Aunt Jeanne and Jacob. Inside she found a tack tote filled with grooming tools and supplies. She hugged Aunt Jeanne and patted Jacob, offering him the empty box. "Thank you, Aunt Jeanne. Now I have my own brushes, currycomb and hoof pick when I go to Willow Tree Stable for my lessons. This is perfect!"

Jacob was sitting inside the empty box, satisfied with his gift. The next gift Aunt Jeanne opened was from Julie's parents. Julie knew what it was and tried to be patient as Aunt Jeanne struggled with the ribbon and wrapping paper. "Oh! It's a portable CD player! Just what I've wanted. Now

I can carry my music around with me wherever I go."

"Open the other one, Aunt Julie. It's from me."

Aunt Jeanne unwrapped the five CD set of John Denver's greatest hits. "Am I THAT easy to shop for?" asked Aunt Jeanne.

"I just remember you saying you wished you had some of your favorite albums on CD."

Aunt Jeanne handed Julie the gift from her parents. It was both big and heavy. Jacob's eyes grew large at the size of the box. This one was harder for Julie to open, because she was wishing her parents were here right now. After she took the paper off, it turned out to be the box their new television had come in last month. Aunt Jeanne went to the kitchen and returned with a pair of scissors, to help Julie with the masking tape. When the top was finally opened, Julie screamed. It was a hunt seat saddle!

"I don't believe it! My OWN saddle!" After taking riding lessons once a week for two years, Julie now has her own saddle to polish and clean.

"Can I wake up my parents now?" asked Julie. "I can't wait to thank them!"

"It's still pretty early, kiddo. Why don't you open

this last present?"

Julie almost hadn't noticed the shoebox-sized package with her name on it. And it didn't say whom it was from.

"Maybe it's from Jacob?" offered Aunt Jeanne.

This box was taped shut, too. It took Julie a few minutes to get inside the box. Julie finally removed the top and found a leather halter and matching lead shank.

"OOOH!" exclaimed Julie. "But who is it from?"

Aunt Jeanne smiled. "Look on the halter. Isn't there a nameplate?"

On the halter was a polished brass nameplate. The name "THADDIUS" was engraved in neat block letters.

"Thad is my most favorite school horse," explained Julie. "Our lessons together are always so much fun. But, Aunt Jeanne, Thad already has a halter."

"Well, when I went out to my shed to give him his breakfast this morning, he told me he wanted a new one, so he could look his best for you."

"What? Thad's here?" spluttered Julie.

"Your parents bought him last week. When they couldn't get home for Christmas, your father called Willow Tree Stable and asked them to haul Thad here early this morning. They'll come back for him after supper. But when he goes back to the stable, his stall will have your name on it, too. NOW you can call your folks!"

# Boomer

"And in sixth place in Pony Pleasure today, we have Karen Murphy on Jack's Bonanza," called the announcer. Karen rode to the gate and accepted her ribbon. That left Mike and his pony alone in the center of the arena.

"That's okay, Boomer," Mike said as he patted his sturdy black pony. "We tried our best."

Aunt Jenny was waiting for them at the arena gate. "You and Boomer did a fine job. I can't believe this is your first horse show!"

"Boomer and I tried really hard, Aunt Jenny," said Mike. "But we only get to practice together when I come for the summer. I wish we had won a ribbon. Boomer is such a great pony. He deserves a ribbon!"

Aunt Jenny smiled. "I couldn't part with Boomer when your cousin Ken got too big for him. I'm so glad you like riding."

Mike dismounted and led Boomer back to the horse trailer. "What do we have next, Aunt Jenny?" asked Mike. "Are we almost done?"

"The last event is called Trail Class. Tie Boomer to the trailer and loosen his girth. We'll go watch some others go through the course."

"But I didn't practice for a Trail Class, Aunt Jenny. What do I do?"

Aunt Jenny just kept smiling as they walked across the field to the Trail event. Mike couldn't believe his eyes! In front of him was an obstacle course for horses and riders.

One at a time, horse and rider entered the course. First, the rider had to guide his horse through an L-shaped path with logs on both sides. Then the rider had to guide the horse backward through the L. Some horses did it easily. Other horses refused to back up or stepped over the log.

"The judge scores each horse and rider for every obstacle," explained Aunt Jenny. "Then the pair with the highest score wins. I entered you and Boomer in the pony division. Just watch for a little while, then we'll get you and Boomer ready to go."

Mike loved trail riding at Aunt Jenny's farm.

On his summer visits he rode Boomer nearly every day. But he wasn't so sure about riding alone in front of such a big crowd.

"I don't know, Aunt Jenny. It looks pretty hard. Do I have to do it?" asked Mike.

"Of course not," replied Aunt Jenny. How about just watching for a little while before you decide? Sound fair?"

"Deal!" answered Mike.

Mike watched as a man on a big red Quarter Horse entered the trail course. His horse walked through the L and backed neatly out of it. At the next obstacle, the man rode up to a mailbox, opened and closed the mailbox door and then put up the flag. "That doesn't look so hard," Mike told Aunt Jenny. But the next rider to come along couldn't get her horse to stand still at the mailbox, so she never got the flag up. At the third obstacle, her horse stood neatly as she stopped and put on a bright yellow raincoat.

Most of the horses and riders were able to open and close the gate at the fourth obstacle. But several horses refused to walk over the little man-made bridge at the next obstacle. Mike watched closely as the next horse and rider trotted over the set of poles laying on the ground. He began to think that maybe he and Boomer could do this.

"I'll try Aunt Jenny," decided Mike. "Boomer and I always have a great time riding the trails at your farm. I bet he'll try hard for me. But after the poles on the ground, the next part looks hard. Most of the big horses are just stepping over the big log. I don't think Boomer and I can do it."

"The rules don't say you have to walk over it, Mike. It just says you need to cross it. If you keep trotting after the poles, Boomer will jump over it. Haven't you jumped over logs like that on the trail before?"

"Sure," answered Mike. "But never with anybody watching. Plus, we can't see what the last obstacle is. They've got it inside that big horse trailer. And it must be spooky. Almost every single horse has backed out looking scared."

"It's up to you, then," said Aunt Jenny. "You and Boomer."

Mike closed his eyes and decided. "Okay, we'll try it, Aunt Jenny. We haven't gotten a ribbon all day and that's not why I love Boomer anyway."

Boomer's girth was tightened and they were ready to go in just a few minutes. Aunt Jenny pinned the number 44 on Mike's back and helped him mount up. At the arena, there were five riders ahead of him before it was his turn. Mike watched each horse and rider pair closely. Each horse seemed to have a problem with at least one of the obstacles.

"Rider number 59 is next," called a man with a clipboard. "Then comes rider number 44."

"That's us, Boomer. It's almost our turn," said Mike, as he patted Boomer's neck.

"Just try your best," said Aunt Jenny. "And have some fun."

"Okay, let's have rider number 44," called the man with the clipboard.

Mike rode Boomer up to the gate and tipped his hat. Aunt Jenny smiled and gave him thumbs up.

"Good luck, son," offered the clipboard man as they entered the ring.

First Mike and Boomer came to the L made of logs. Mike steered Boomer through L-shaped path. Then Mike backed Boomer out, just they way they came in. "Thank you," said the first judge. She smiled and wrote a score down on her clipboard.

Next came the mailbox. Because Boomer was

a pony, Mike reached the mailbox easily. Boomer stood quietly as Mike opened and closed the mailbox door and raised the flag. "Very nice, young man," said the next judge as he wrote on his clipboard. Mike let the reins rest on Boomer's neck as he put on the yellow raincoat at the next obstacle. Boomer turned around to look at Mike to see what was going on, but he never moved a hoof. "Okay," the raincoat judge said as she wrote on her clipboard.

Next came the gate. Mike had been thinking about how to open and close the gate. He decided to ride up to it and unlatch the gate with his right hand. Then he guided Boomer through the gate as it opened. After they were through, Mike turned Boomer and had him turn on his haunches and then walk forward a few steps so he could re-latch the gate. "Good thinking," said the gate judge.

When they came to the little bridge, Boomer stopped. Then he put one hoof on the bridge. Mike patted his neck. "Good boy, Boomer. You can do it." Boomer took the cue and walked proudly across the wooden bridge as his hooves tapped with each step. "Well done," smiled the bridge judge.

Mike asked Boomer to trot as they came to the poles on the ground. Together they trotted easily over the poles and continued toward the big log. Just before the log, Mike squeezed his legs and leaned forward in the saddle. Boomer jumped the log with inches to spare. Folks watching from the side clapped for the pony and his rider.

At the last obstacle, the judge asked Mike to dismount. "Please lead your pony into the trailer and then back him out," instructed the judge.

Mike dismounted holding Boomer's reins. As he led Boomer up to the trailer, he couldn't believe what he saw. Inside the horse trailer was a large white turkey in a cage! "No wonder the other horses were scared," Mike thought to himself. "I'd be scared, too!"

Boomer looked inside the trailer and put one hoof up and stepped in. Then he saw the turkey. The turkey must have had quite enough of this horse nonsense. He gobbled loudly and puffed up his feathers to look even bigger. Boomer just stood there, not moving a muscle. Now what? thought Mike. That was all Mike had time for. Boomer stepped all the way into the trailer and right up to the turkey cage. The turkey gobbled again. Boomer put his nose right up to the cage to get a better look at the bird. The turkey gobbled for the third time. Boomer nickered softly to the turkey and backed slowly out of the trailer. The judge tried hard not to laugh as he wrote down Mike's last score.

Mike led Boomer back to their horse trailer. Aunt Jenny ran to meet them. "I'm so proud of you both. What a great job! You and Boomer are a perfect team."

When the announcer read the Trail Class awards, everyone clapped for Mike and Boomer as they rode up to collect their 1st place ribbon and trophy.

"Boomer's just the best pony ever," Mike told Aunt Jenny on the way home from the horse show.

"I'm so glad you think so, Mike. I talked with your folks yesterday and they are going to board Boomer at a riding stable near your house. You'll be taking him home with you at the end of the summer. That is, if it's okay with you."

"Are you kidding?" Mike exclaimed. "I'm the luckiest kid I know!

# Cody

Ten-year-old Sarah Kingsley loved her pony more than anything in the world. Sarah shook her long red braids as she exclaimed: "Hold still, Cody. I'm almost done braiding your tail. With your mane and tail braided like that, you look elegant. This must be what it was like for Mom when I was little and she brushed and braided my hair." Sarah was putting the finishing touches on her pony, getting him ready for their first horse show. She had already washed, combed, brushed and polished the stout little Welsh pony until he shined. His sorrel body glowed in contrast to the white sock on his left hind foot.

"Today we are going to show everyone how hard we have been working since last fall," Sarah said to Cody.

Indeed, Sarah and Cody had practiced many hours to get ready for this horse show today. There would be many expensive and professionally trained horses and ponies at the show, as well as horses and riders decked out in expensive tack and show clothes. Sarah loved her pony, and wouldn't trade him. She just wanted to do her best.

Sarah's dad bought Cody last fall for $600. She had wanted a pony for as long as she could remember. When Cody backed calmly out of the trailer and her dad put the lead rope in her hand last September, Sarah knew her dream had really come true.

Before loading him in the small red horse trailer, Sarah carefully wrapped each of Cody's legs in green polo wraps. This would help protect him from bumping or scraping his legs during the trip to the show grounds. As a finishing touch, she covered him with his green sheet. This would hopefully keep him clean until they got to the show.

"Ready to load him, Sarah?" asked her father.

"He's all set to go, Dad! Did you remember to put a bale of hay in the truck?"

"I'm sure we have everything Cody needs, honey. You never forget anything when it comes to that pony. But what about you? Do you have everything YOU need?"

Sarah's mom came from the house holding a black velvet-covered helmet in her hand. "You won't do much showing today without this!" she exclaimed.

"Oops! Thanks, for remembering, Mom. It's just that I'm so excited about our first show!"

With a little encouragement from Sarah, Cody neatly stepped up into the trailer. Sarah snapped the short trailer tie to his halter and climbed out of the small side door. By the time she got around to the back of the trailer, her father had already closed the rear door and locked it securely.

"All right, ladies," announced Sarah's father. "Anyone going to the annual 4-H horse show had better get in the truck right now!"

Sarah jumped into the middle spot of the front seat and buckled herself. She rode between her parents with her riding helmet on her lap. She wasn't going to forget it a second time.

The twenty-minute ride to the show grounds suddenly seemed very short to Sarah. This was her first real horse show with her own pony. All of a sudden, she wasn't sure she was ready. "Cody is ready," she thought to herself. "I hope I don't let him down."

They had arrived early enough that Sarah's father pulled the truck and trailer into the first row. Sarah's stomach was feeling a little tight as they all got out of the truck.

"This is great," said Sarah's mother. "Now you won't have to walk very far to get back to the trailer between classes."

Sarah started to wish she had stayed home and practiced more before trying a horse show. Her father opened the trailer door and Cody backed out, looking around in wonder. He didn't seem to be afraid, just curious about his new surroundings. Sarah patted his neck reassuringly, mostly reassuring herself. It worked. As soon as she began taking off his leg wraps and rubbing him one more time with a soft cloth, she regained some confidence.

"I love you, Cody," she told the stocky pony. "Whatever else happens today, we'll have tried our best and you'll still be my pony."

Sarah's mother returned from the entry booth with a show bill and Sarah's back number. "I got you number 10 for good luck," said her mother.

"And in case the judge asks you your back number, you shouldn't forget this one."

Sarah looked at the show bill. Her first class was Pony Showmanship. There were three classes before her, so she took off Cody's halter and put his English bridle on him. As she and Cody started to walk up to the show ring, her mother called to her.

"Wait, honey! You forgot to let me pin your number onto your jacket."

Sarah tried to stand still as her mother patiently pinned her back number onto her hunt coat. Cody was also anxious to get going and started to pull on the reins. Sarah's dad took Cody's reins so her mom could make the finishing touches. "Your hair looks so nice and neat in a French braid. Let me add your helmet and you will be all set to enter the ring," said her mother.

Sarah's dad handed the pony's reins back to his daughter. "You and Cody should go watch some of the older kids do their showmanship class. That will keep you from thinking too much and getting nervous."

Sarah was really impressed as she watched some of the beautiful horses and their owners do their showmanship patterns. One at a time, each rider led his or her horse to the judge at a walk. Halt. Set up square for inspection. Turn on the haunches. Trot back toward the line. Halt. 360-degree turn. Trot through the line. Set up square and wait.

Sarah was really worried that the pattern for her showmanship class might have a 360-degree turn. They hadn't practiced that. She decided to take Cody over to the makeup area and try one now. Cody didn't understand what Sarah was asking. Every time she put pressure on the reins she held under his chin, he backed up five steps. Too late now, she decided.

As the announcer asked the Pony Showmanship entrants to lead their ponies in at a walk, Sarah suddenly noticed how many other ponies were waiting to go in. Sarah counted at least ten other ponies. Ribbons were only awarded for the first six places. Not everyone would leave with a ribbon today.

As Sarah and Cody approached the in-gate, her father called to her, "Smile, Sarah. Just do your best."

The ringmaster asked each contestant to line their pony up next to one another in the center of the arena. The judge walked up and smiled as she said: "Here is your pattern today. I want you to trot out of line to me, halt and set up for inspection. I will ask you a horsemanship question. Then turn your pony 180 degrees and walk back to your place in line. Halt. Then back your pony five steps. Any questions?"

The first pony didn't want to trot right away, but seemed to get everything else perfect. Except for the back. He didn't want to back up. He swung his rump to the side.

The next pony trotted for his owner, but wouldn't set his feet squarely for the judge. Sarah watched and held her breath as it came close to her turn.

Trotting briskly from the line, Cody stayed next to Sarah and stopped squarely in front of the judge. Amazed and proud, Sarah smiled and presented Cody for inspection.

"Can you tell me the name of the bony patch found behind the fetlock?" asked the judge. Sarah thought hard.

"The ergot?" she answered hopefully.

"Thank you," said the judge. "Please complete your pattern." The judge gave no clue if she had answered the question correctly.

Back in line, Sarah continued to watch as other ponies and their owners completed the showmanship pattern.

A girl leading a sorrel and white paint pony went last. Every move was perfectly executed.

"They were awesome," Sarah told Cody in a quiet voice.

The judge asked each contestant to turn and display their back number. She marked the placings on her clipboard and walked to the announcer's booth.

As the announcer read the placings, Sarah was a little disappointed. She didn't get 6th, 5th, 4th or 3rd place. She thought Cody had done a good job, especially for his first show. She wasn't listening when the announcer called her name and number for 2nd place.

"Aren't you number 10?" asked the boy next to her. "Don't you want your 2nd place ribbon?"

Sarah and Cody thanked the young girl at the gate that was handing out the ribbons. Sarah pinned the bright red ribbon on Cody's bridle and hugged him. The girl with the awesome paint pony walked by carrying the blue ribbon.

"Congratulations," she told Sarah. "I can see I'm going to have to really practice if I want to keep ahead of you two!"

# It's a Small World

"This year's theme for costume class at the county fair will be?" Mrs. Wilson paused dramatically, "It's a Small World After All!"

The 4-H members crowded around her began to buzz with excitement.

"This sounds like fun," said Betsy. "I know what I'm going to do already."

"Oh, I don't know. It might be hard to decide. I can think of at least three neat ideas already," said Maria. "What about you, Linda? What are you and Waldo going to do?"

"I'm not sure I'm going to enter costume class," confessed Linda. "I'll think about, though." Linda stood quietly as the kids around her wandered away in small group. "I wish I wasn't so shy," Linda thought to herself. "I'd like to enter the costume class, but I don't have any idea what I could do."

Linda had always been shy. Unless she was with her large palomino pony. Waldo stood an inch too short at the withers to be classified as a "horse." Linda did not mind at all that Waldo was a "pony." He was her pony.

"Let's go, squirt," called her brother Mike. "I've got plenty to do besides drive you to a 4-H meeting!" He tried to look impatient, but his big grin gave him away.

Everyone turned to look when Mike called out, then turned again to see who he was calling a "squirt." Linda's cheeks turned pink with embarrassment as some of her friends giggled. "Why does he have to be so loud?" Linda thought silently. "He makes me crazy!"

As she climbed into the passenger seat, she told him: "I'm not a squirt, Mike. Stop saying that, especially in front of my friends. It's embarassing."

"Aw, lighten up, Sis! You know I'm just kidding. Besides, you are my "little" sister. You should be used to it by now."

"I'm not like you, Mike. I don't like having everyone looking at me," answered Linda.

"Yeah, I know. You're shy. Except when you're

riding that pony of yours!" Mike responded. "You're always asking Mom or Dad or me to watch something amazing Waldo can do."

"But it's different when I'm with Waldo. We're a team. I don't feel awkward or shy when we're together."

Linda rode quietly the rest of the way home, lost in thought. Mike sang along with the car radio in his usual booming voice, pretending not to notice his sister's silence. Mike turned into their driveway and turned off the ignition, saying: "Okay, give."

"Give what?" asked Linda.

"What I mean is give it up! Tell me what you've been thinking about most of the way home. Are you mad at me? I'm sorry if I hurt your feelings, kiddo."

Finally, Linda spoke: "No, that's not it at all, Mike. I'm not mad at you. You're right, I should be used to your teasing by now. My problem is the county fair next week. I sort of want to enter the costume class with Waldo, but I don't know if I have the nerve."

"I should have realized it had something to do with that darn pony. Do you think about anything else?" Linda had to smile at her brother. He cer- tainly knew her well. She loved her crazy brother, wishing she could be a little more like him.

"Costume class? Piece of cake," exclaimed Mike. You could wear my really awesome Frankenstein mask and Waldo could be your assistant, Igor."

"No, no. You don't understand, Mike. They have a theme every year. This year's theme is called *It's a Small World After All.* You know, like the ride at Disney World®. If I do enter, I've got to come up with a costume that represents a country or nationality or something. I'm sure Betsy's going to use Scotland, since her mom plays the bag-pipes. She'll probably make her horse wear a kilt!"

"Well, you've got a week. You'll think of something, Sis."

Five days later, Linda still needed an idea. She had thought of (and rejected) at least ten ideas already. Some were just too hard to create and others were too expensive to make with her limited budget of $25. Mike came out of the house found her sitting on the back steps.

"Why the long face, Sis?" he asked with big-brotherly concern.

"I still don't have a good idea for the costume class. All my friends have theirs done already. And I'm running out of time. The fair starts day after tomorrow." Linda sighed.

"And you mean you haven't come to your big brother for help? Come on! You know my reputation for Halloween costumes. I always show up with something out of this world," bragged Mike.

Linda sat up straight and stared at her brother. "Say that again, Mike," insisted Linda.

"Say what? You should have come to me for help?"

"No. I mean the part about being out of this world. I think I might have an idea. What if I forgot about doing a nationality and made Waldo into an alien? You know, like from Mars. What do you think?"

"Hey, cool!" answered Mike. "We could dress you like a NASA astronaut. It could work! You could bring Waldo back from Mars and say it really IS a small world after all!"

"Okay, I think maybe I could do it. But could I wear your snowmobile helmet? Then people really won't be able to see my face."

"Sure you can wear my helmet," said Mike. "I'll put the plastic face shield on it. And you could wear Dad's painting jumpsuit. We'll put a patch that says NASA on the pocket. The best part is that you haven't spent any money yet. You can spend all your budget on Waldo."

"I'm with you so far, big brother. But how do I transform Waldo into an alien?"

"That," said Mike, "you need to leave to the king of Halloween! I'm going to ask Mom if we can borrow her car for a trip downtown. I know the perfect place to shop for your project."

Mike parked the car in front of a store called *The White Rabbit.* Elaborate costumes filled the display windows.

"Don't forget that I only have $25," Linda reminded him.

"Just follow me. I know what I'm doing," Mike replied.

Inside the costume shop, the shelves reached the ceiling and were packed with costumes and accessories to complete any outfit. Mike led Linda through the maze of shelves to the back of the shop. He stopped in front of the makeup display.

"Aha! Here it is. Just what we need," Mike exclaimed as he handed a can of hair spray to his sister.

"What's this?" asked Linda. "It looks like hair spray."

"Look closer. Look at the color on the label," said Mike.

"Bright Green," Linda read aloud. "Bright green? You don't mean...?"

"Yup. I think we could spray Waldo green. He's palomino, so we should be able to turn him green pretty easily. Don't worry. I promise that it washes right off. Don't you remember when I sprayed my hair red for Valentine's Day last year?"

"But it sure would take a lot of this stuff," replied Linda.

"Yeah, I bet we would need 10 cans or so. This stuff only costs $1.95 per can, so you would still stay within your budget. Do you think Waldo would let us spray him?"

"I think so," Linda answered. "It would probably sound like fly spray to him. Waldo doesn't mind that. But it would take a long time to turn him green from nose to tail."

"No problem, Sis. I'll help you. A green pony is something I've got to see!"

Unfortunately, it turned out there were only eight cans of green hair spray. They asked the clerk, but she said that all they had was already out on the shelf. "This might not be enough, Mike. What can we do?"

"It depends. How crazy are you willing to be?" asked her brother.

Linda had to laugh. "Do you realize how that sounds? We're already talking about spraying a pony green. What does crazy have to do with it now?"

"Well, what if we get another color of hair spray, too? We could make his beautiful blond mane and tail a lovely shade of purple," suggested Mike.

"I can't believe I'm even considering this. I'm not sure if you're a good influence on me, Mike!"

At the register, Linda paid for eight cans of green and two cans of purple hair spray. The cashier didn't bat an eye. Evidently, she had learned not to ask questions when folks shopped at *The White Rabbit.*

Two days later, the county fair was underway. Adults and children strolled through the livestock barns, inspecting the variety of chickens, goats, turkeys, rabbits, pigs, cattle and horses. "Don't miss the 4-H costume class, folks," came the voice over the loudspeaker. "Horses and their riders like you've never seen them before. The action begins at 1:00 p.m. today at the main livestock arena."

Linda sat on a bale of hay, eating her sandwich. "I'd better finish this quick lunch and get start getting ready," she told herself.

"The cavalry has arrived," announced her brother Mike. He was carrying a huge cardboard box. "We've only got 2 hours to perform this magic. Let's get going. But first, I need to do something."

Mike pulled an old bedsheet out of the box he had brought. He used thumbtacks to hang across the front of Waldo's stall. "This is a top-secret operation," he explained. "We don't want anyone seeing Waldo until he's ready!"

Mike held up the sheet so he and Linda could step inside Waldo's box stall. Waldo was curious and started nosing around the cardboard box.

"Be patient, Waldo," said Linda as she snapped

a lead rope on his halter and tied it to the stall post. "We haven't even gotten started yet." She fed him a carrot as a peace offering.

Linda took a can of green hair spray from the box and read the directions. "Shake well before use. Okay, Mike. Grab a can and let's see what happens. Just remember, this was your idea!"

Mike grabbed another can of green hair spray and shook it enthusiastically. "Let's try spraying his rump first," suggested Mike. "Then he won't be able to see exactly what we're doing to him!"

Waldo didn't seem to mind the attention and the spraying, as long as he got a carrot once in a while. Soon his light yellow coat was a peculiar shade of green.

"Okay, he's definitely green," Mike announced. "You'd better take off and get into your astronaut outfit. I think I can handle making his mane and tail purple."

"All right" said Linda. "But you had better promise not to spray anything else purple!"

Fifteen minutes later, Linda stepped out of the bathroom as Commander Linda Walker. The NASA emblem was visible on her uniform pocket. She put on the helmet and pulled down the face shield as she walked back to Waldo's stall. When she stepped behind the sheet, she was unprepared for what greeted her. Waldo was green. His mane and tail were purple. But, somehow he had also acquired string mop-heads on each leg and they had also been sprayed purple.

"What is this?" she exclaimed. "The Clydesdale from Mars?"

"I thought you should be surprised, too," Mike explained with a grin. "Duct tape will hold them in place. Don't you think he looks great?"

"Well, I suppose that's one word for it. What have I gotten myself into?"

As Linda offered Waldo yet another carrot, the voice over the loudspeaker announced: "The 4-H equine costume class begins in 15 minutes. Contestants please be ready to enter the ring."

"Too late to change your mind now, kiddo," said Mike. "It's show time!"

Mike took down the sheet and held the stall door open. Waldo hesitated, then took a couple of small steps. He looked at Linda and cocked his head.

"I don't know who looks crazier," said Linda

from inside the helmet.

Waldo seemed reassured by Linda's voice and followed alongside her, raising each leg high off the ground with each step.

"Look, mom! A green horse," exclaimed a young boy. "Cool."

Everyone turned to look at the alien and his companion. Linda took a deep breath and closed her eyes. Please, she thought silently. Make me invisible!

A crowd of curious spectators followed Linda and Waldo to the show arena. Mike grabbed his camera and followed to record the moment. Linda could see that the grandstand was full. Her stomach felt like it was full of dancing butterflies.

"You can do it, Sis," said Mike, placing his hand on her shoulder. "Time for blastoff!"

The contestants and their horses entered the arena as the loudspeaker played *It's a Small World After All*. Soon the arena looked like a meeting of the United Nations. A Dutch girl rode on a horse wearing a gigantic wooden shoe. Linda's friend Betsy carried a bagpipe, wearing a plaid Scottish kilt just like the one her horse was wearing on his front quarters. The horse and

rider that followed seemed to be from the Alps, complete with matching lederhosen and green Tiroler hats. An Arabian sheik, complete with flowing robes, sat regally upon his mount. Pocahontas joined them on a black-and-white paint pony with a red hand-print on his rump.
A Spanish señorita rode in, followed by a Canadian mountie. A boy dressed in red-white-and-blue and wearing a feather in his cap (who seemed to be Yankee Doodle) rode in on a pony everyone guessed must be named Macaroni.

Then came Linda and Waldo.

As Waldo lifted each foot carefully, the audience laughed out loud. His shaggy purple fetlocks only added to his already comical appearance. From inside her helmet, Linda looked out at the crowd and took another deep breath. Then she saw Mike waving at her from the first row. Camera in hand, he was waving and smiling and trying to take her picture, all at the same time. "He looks pretty silly, too," Linda told herself.

More colorful horses and costumes followed, until the arena was full. The sixteen contestants continued to parade around the arena until the music stopped. The crowd applauded as they

lined up in the center of the ring.

The judge walked up to each contestant, carrying his clipboard. He greeted each contestant individually and inquired about his or her costume. When it was Linda's turn, she looked out to find Mike. He gave her a big grin and a thumb's up.

"Hello," began the judge. "May I ask who you are?"

"My name is Commander Linda Wilson, sir. I've just returned from a special mission to Mars. Since I was able to locate intelligent life there, I brought Waldo back as proof."

The judge was speechless. Then he roared with laughter. Although they couldn't hear what Linda had said, the crowd clapped its approval of the green pony and his owner.

When it was time to announce the winners, the judge was given a microphone. "This is always a hard class to judge. Everyone here has worked so hard. Let's give them all a round of applause, shall we?" Next, the judge read the placing from his clipboard. "For most authentic costume, our winner today is Allison James on Chiquita." The Spanish señorita rode up to accept her blue ribbon amid enthusiastic applause. "Now we have the award for the most creative use of materials. Our winner today is Paul Corning." The Arab sheik on his gray Arabian waved as they trotted and jingled to the judge to accept his blue ribbon.

"And, the award for the most humorous costume goes to Linda Walker and Waldo. Linda explained that she's just returned from Mars and that it really is a small world after all!" The crowd clapped and gave her a standing ovation as she and Waldo came forward to accept their prize.

Afterwards, as she scrubbed Waldo back to his normal color, she smiled at her accomplishment. It wasn't the blue ribbon that made her smile. That was just a special bonus. No, today was much more than that. It was Mike's help and encouragement. Plus, the fact that she went through with the whole crazy thing. In the end, it wasn't as hard as she thought. And, her brother could be really terrific when he chose to be.

# Winnie

"Mom, the mailman's here!" hollered Winnie as she looked out the front window. Winnie was excited because that usually meant there was something too big to fit in the mailbox.

When the letter carrier knocked, Winnie ran to answer the door. Mr. Arnold wasn't holding a package and he looked concerned. "Is your mom home?" he asked.

"She'll be right here. Would you like to come in and wait for her?"

Winnie's mother came into the living room carrying a basket of laundry."Hello, Mr. Arnold," she said as she set the basket down. "What brings you down our long driveway?"

Mr. Arnold frowned. "It's your neighbor, Mrs. Watson. I thought it was odd that yesterday's mail was still in her box when I made the delivery today. I drove up to her house and found her hobbling around with a cane. She said she twisted her knee day before yesterday."

"Oh, I wish she had called," said Winnie's mother, sounding worried.

"She's always been pretty independent and doesn't want to be any trouble," said Mr. Arnold. "That's why I stopped by to let you know. I thought you and Winnie could look in on her and see if she needs anything."

"I'm so glad you let us know, Mr. Arnold. Winnie and I will go over there right after lunch."

Their noisy blue truck rumbled as they drove up Mrs. Watson's long driveway. Winnie jumped out of the passenger side and ran up to the back porch. Winnie's mother followed with a picnic basket.

Sitting on her sun porch, Mrs. Watson looked

up from her knitting and greeted them.

"Hello, ladies. Looks like Mr. Arnold tattled on me," said the white-haired woman.

"Yup," answered Winnie. "He told us you could use a visit. And we brought you supper."

"Well, thank you," said Mrs. Watson. "I told him I'd get by. I do appreciate your kindness. but I'm more worried about how all my animals are going to get their supper. I'm still not getting around very well."

"Aha," exclaimed Winnie's mother. "What if you make a list for Winnie? You and I can visit while Winnie helps with your chores."

Winnie jumped up. "I don't need a list. Feed the chickens, fill the cat's dish, make sure the rabbit has food and water and feed Jake his hay and grain. Did I forget anything?"

"That's pretty good, Winnie," said Mrs. Watson with a smile. "I'm going to take you up on your offer. You'll find everything you need in the feed room."

"I wish you were that anxious to do your chores at home," said Winnie's mother, laughing.

"Come on, Mom. Cleaning my room isn't anything like feeding animals! I'd rather be outside any day!"

"Do they still use the word tomboy?" asked Winnie's mother. "I sure seem to have one at my house."

Winnie headed for the barn, eager to help. After the chickens, cat and rabbit were fed, Winnie looked behind the barn for Jake. The huge black horse was standing on three feet, resting the fourth, head down and napping in the late afternoon sun.

"Hey Jake," called Winnie. "I'm in charge of supper tonight. You'd better wake up if you want yours!"

Jake lifted his head and watched Winnie disappear back into the barn. By the time the Percheron made his way to his stall, his hay and grain were already waiting for him.

"You are such a cool horse, Jake," said Winnie as she watched the gelding munch his supper. "I'm glad Mrs. Watson kept you."

Jake had been Mr. Watson's favorite horse. Dressed as farmer from the 1880's, Mr. Watson hitched Jake to the buckboard wagon and proudly drove him in the Old Fashioned Days parade every summer. When her husband died last fall, Mrs. Watson sold the two younger horse teams, but she didn't have the heart to sell Jake.

"Everybody's fed," reported Winnie. "It was fun! Can I come back tomorrow morning and help again?"

"That's a great idea, Winnie," said her mother. You could ride your bike over after you clean your room."

The next morning Winnie hopped on her bike and headed for the Watson farm. As Winnie parked her bike in front of the barn, she saw Mrs. Watson smile and wave from her kitchen window.

After she finished feeding all the animals, she headed for the house to report to Mrs. Watson.

"Everybody's fed and watered, Mrs. Watson."

Mrs. Watson laid her knitting in her lap. "I sure appreciate your help, Winnie. I hope you'll stay and visit for a little while," said Mrs. Watson.

"Sure," said Winnie, "As long as you don't think you're going to teach me how to knit. I'm all thumbs!"

"Actually, I usually do most of my knitting during winter. I like being outside in my garden in the summer. But it's nice to have something to do with my hands while I wait for my knee to get better."

"How did you hurt your knee, anyway?" asked Winnie.

"Can you keep a secret? I was trying to move the wagon and see if I could hitch Jake up myself," confessed Mrs. Watson.

"By yourself? Why?" Winnie was amazed.

"I was hoping I could drive him in the Old Fashioned Days parade next month," said Mrs. Watson. "It was always Mr. Watson's favorite summer event. I like dressing up in my long dress and bonnet. It reminds me of my grand-mother. And I know how to hitch and drive the wagon."

"I won't tell," said Winnie. "Just make sure you don't try it by yourself again."

After finishing her lemonade, Winnie went to the mailbox and brought Mrs. Watson her mail.

"Here's the entry form for the Old Fashioned Days parade," said Mrs. Watson as she sorted the mail.

Suddenly, Winnie got an idea. "I gotta go right now, Mrs. Watson. You just rest your knee," said

Winnie as she jumped up from her chair.

Before she left, Winnie brought Mrs. Watson a glass of lemonade and promised to return for evening chores.

"I'm home, Mom," called Winnie as she came in the house. She found her mother reading the newspaper in the living room. Winnie sat down next to her on the couch. "Mom, remember how I said I didn't want to dress up for Old Fashioned Days?" asked Winnie.

"Yes, how could I forget?" answered her mother. "You said you wouldn't be seen in public wearing the dress and bonnet I made for you. I have to admit, I was pretty disappointed."

"Well, what if I've changed my mind?"

"Oh really?" said her mother. "What do you have in mind?"

"I got the idea from Mrs. Watson. She wants to drive Jake in the parade. I thought maybe I could help and ride in the parade with her. Then I wouldn't feel so silly in the dress. I'm still not convinced about the bonnet, though. What do you think? Could I ask Mrs. Watson?"

"I'll think about it. How about if I go with you after supper and we'll discuss it with her?"

That evening, Mrs. Watson was surprised to see Winnie jump out of the truck in a bonnet and long gingham dress. "What do you think of my pioneer daughter?" asked Winnie's mother.

"You look perfectly lovely, Winnie!" exclaimed Mrs. Watson.

"I'm practicing for Old Fashioned Days. Now all I need is a ride for the parade. Can I get a ride with you and Jake?"

"With Jake and me?" asked Mrs. Watson. "I don't think my knee will be better by then. Maybe we can do it next year."

"Couldn't you teach me how to hitch Jake to the wagon? Then you could drive him in the parade. I'd even wear this dress if I could ride in the wagon with you!"

"It's up to you, Mrs. Watson," said Winnie's mother. "If you'd like Winnie's help, it's fine with me. And it would be a special treat to see her wearing a dress in public!"

"Well, let's give it a try," said Mrs. Watson. "We have a month to practice. But first, Jake's harness needs to be cleaned and oiled. You sure can't work on the harness in that lovely dress. Make sure you're wearing old clothes when you come back tomorrow morning. Even working together, it will take us a few hours to do the entire harness."

"I'll ride my bike over tomorrow, right after breakfast," promised Winnie.

Winnie raced through her feeding chores for Mrs. Watson the next morning. Jake's harness was hanging on the tack room wall. She used the wheelbarrow to bring all the harness pieces up to the house. Mrs. Watson sat on the porch and supervised as Winnie cleaned and oiled all the leather pieces. Mrs. Watson polished the brass on the collar. By the time they were through cleaning Jake's harness, it was almost time for lunch.

"Thought you ladies might be hungry by now," called Winnie's mother from the front yard. "I've brought lunch, so I hope you're ready to take a break."

"We're done," Winnie proclaimed. "Now that the harness is ready, when can we try it on Jake?" she asked.

"Not until you've eaten lunch," said her mother.

"Yes, I'm ready to take a break," Mrs. Watson said. "Jake can wait to try on his harness until after we've had lunch."

Winnie ate quickly and finished her lunch in a matter of minutes. Her mother and Mrs. Watson were still eating.

"I'll just go out and brush Jake while you two finish your lunch," said Winnie as she raced out the back door.

Winnie put the harness back in the wheelbarrow and took it back to the barn. She put Jake's halter on him and led him to the crossties in the barn. Jake stood patiently between the two large posts as Winnie curried and brushed him from nose to tail. She had to stand on a bale of hay to comb his mane and forelock.

Soon her mother and Mrs. Watson joined her. Mrs. Watson walked slowly, using her cane. Winnie's mother brought a lawn chair, which she set up a few feet away from Jake. Mrs. Watson settled comfortably in the lawn chair, ready to give directions.

"I'll leave you two to your task, I'm going to take care of our lunch dishes," said Winnie's mother, as she disappeared through the barn door.

"Okay, Winnie. The first thing you need to remember is to take your time. We're in no hurry. Every buckle and snap on the entire harness must be fastened correctly. Once Jake is hooked to the wagon, it will be too late to discover you missed something," instructed Mrs. Watson.

"I understand," answered Winnie. "Safety first!" Winnie patiently followed Mrs. Watson's step-by-step instructions, tightening straps and fastening buckles. Jake continued to stand still as Winnie checked the last strap and ran the long reins through the rings on the collar. The entire process lasted almost 45 minutes.

"Ta da!" Winnie announced proudly. "I think it's all set."

"Pretty darn good for a first try, Winnie. Are you sure you haven't done this before?" asked Mrs. Watson.

"You just give good directions," said Winnie. "And it helps when you get to work with such a super horse!"

"Yes, Jake is a special horse. And he's done enough for today. Let's have you unharness him now, and we'll practice again tomorrow. After a few more practice sessions, we'll hitch him up and see how he goes for us."

Soon Winnie could harness Jake in only 30 minutes. But she needed some extra help for the next stage. "Mom, can you give me a ride over to Mrs. Watson's house after lunch," Winnie asked.

"Sure. Don't you want to ride your bike?" asked her mother.

"Well, I need more than a ride today. I need a little help getting the wagon out of the barn. It's not super-heavy or anything, but it's really a two-person job."

With her mother's assistance, they were able to lift the wagon shafts and guide it out of the barn. Mrs. Watson was sitting outside in her lawn chair.

"Hmmm. The wagon looks okay," announced Mrs. Watson. "But it sure is going to need a good bath before we'll be able to ride in it!"

Winnie got a bucket and scrub brush from the barn. Her mother retrieved a bottle of liquid dish soap from Mrs. Watson's kitchen. Winnie went to work. After scrubbing and rinsing the entire wagon, Winnie was exhausted.

"Don't worry, we're done for today," said Mrs. Watson. We'll let the wagon dry and try to hitch Jake up tomorrow."

Tomorrow couldn't arrive soon enough for Winnie. She got up extra early and rode her bike to Mrs. Watson's house. She wanted to make sure

Jake was all spiffed up for their first wagon attempt!

By the time Mrs. Watson and Winnie's mother arrived in front of the barn, Jake was already wearing the harness and collar. His ears perked up when Winnie led him to the wagon. Winnie noticed that Mrs. Watson was wearing delicate deerskin gloves.

"What are the gloves for?" she asked.

"Oh, a proper lady always wears gloves for driving," answered Mrs. Watson. "I can't wait to give you two ladies a ride in the wagon."

Winnie backed Jake between the shafts. Her mother held Jake's bridle as Winnie connected Jake's harness to the wagon. When Mrs. Watson was satisfied that everything had been double-checked, she was ready to climb aboard. Winnie held Jake's bridle as her mother helped Mrs. Watson climb carefully into the wagon. Mrs. Watson picked up the reins and smiled.

"Get up, Jake," she called. Jake turned an ear back to listen. "Hey, I'm not kidding. Get up, Jake," she called a second time. Jake stepped out and leaned into the harness. As he walked along the farm lane, he made pulling the big wagon look easy.

"After all your hard work, I think you deserve a ride, Winnie," called Mrs. Watson. "Your mother can hold Jake's bridle while you climb up here beside me."

Riding in the wagon, Winnie could imagine herself living on the prairie a hundred years ago. This is how people traveled, she thought. No cars, no trucks, no school buses.

After the wagon ride, Winnie unhitched Jake and led him to the barn to be unharnessed. When she returned, she found her mother and Mrs. Watson laughing.

"What's so funny?" she asked.

"It's just so wonderful that I'll be able to drive Jake in the parade. If I hadn't hurt me knee, it might not have happened. I guess the joke's on me," said Mrs. Watson.

On the morning of the parade, Winnie brushed Jake until his coat shined like black satin. She got his harness from the tack room and buckled everything in its proper place. With the dirty work out of the way, Winnie went up to Mrs. Watson's house to put on the dress that her mother had made for her.

Mrs. Watson was already in costume. Her bright green bonnet matched her green checked dress. Wearing her deerskin gloves, she held another pair in her hand when Winnie came out in her dress.

"Here is a pair of gloves for you, my dear," said Mrs. Watson. "But where is your bonnet?"

"The bonnet didn't turn out very well, I'm afraid. It was so floppy, I couldn't see where I was going," explained Winnie.

"We can fix that," said Mrs. Watson. "Go in my bedroom and bring me the big green box under my bed." Winnie did as she was told. Inside the box were several bonnets.

"These were made by my grandmother," explained Mrs. Watson. "I'd be thrilled if you wore one of these."

Winnie touched the yellow bonnet gingerly. Yellow was her favorite color.

"Perfect choice," said Mrs. Watson. She tied the bow carefully under Winnie's chin.

It was time to go. They rode into town side-by-side in the horse-drawn wagon. Jake's big hooves clopped out a two-beat rhythm as they trotted along. Arriving at the staging area for the parade, they were assigned a number and waited for their turn to go. Soon Mrs. Watson and Winnie were riding down Main Street, looking like a page from a history book. At a walk, Jake's hooves drummed out 1-2-3-4. 1-2-3-4.

Winnie smiled and waved to the onlookers, looking as if she had just stepped off the prairie. As Mrs. Watson stopped the wagon to wait for the group ahead, Winnie's mother took pictures. What it took to see her daughter in a dress, the world would never know!

# Barney

"I don't want to ride a horse. I don't even want to be here," grumbled Allen.

His foster parents sighed. After two weeks, Allen still hadn't settled in a bit.

"When my grandma gets out of the hospital, she and I can go home and I'll take care of her myself," Allen said.

Mrs. Warner tried to be matter-of-fact. "Your grandma is going to be in the hospital for quite a while, Allen. Even then, her broken hip will probably keep her in a nursing home for a few months. We'll make sure you visit her as much as you want, but you will be staying with us until after Christmas."

Allen stared at his shoes.

"You don't have to learn to ride if you don't want to, Allen," assured Mr. Warner. Our son Randy is away at college, so you can ride his horse Ajax if you want to. We just thought it might be something for you to do this summer. Most of the kids around here have horses."

Allen looked up. "Well, even if I learn to ride a horse, don't expect me to clean stalls or anything like that. I'm not a hired hand, you know."

"I scheduled a riding lesson for you at Twin Pines Stable this Saturday, if you are interested. But I can cancel it if you don't want to go," offered Mrs. Warner.

"Nah, I'll try it once," said Allen. "But don't expect me to love it or anything."

Saturday morning arrived. Allen rode in the truck with Mr. Warner but didn't say a word. As they pulled into the driveway of Twin Pines Stable, Allen could see activity everywhere.

Owners were leading horses of all colors in and out of the barn. Riders were mounted and practicing outside the arena. In the arena, three girls were taking a lesson from a tall young woman.

"Looks like mostly girls to me," complained Allen.

"Don't worry, Allen. Since you are what we call a "novice" rider, we scheduled a private lesson for you. And there are several guys that ride here, too. I'll introduce you to them after your lesson," said Mr. Warner.

Inside the barn, a grandfatherly man in a straw cowboy hat greeted Allen and Mr. Warner. "Howdy, Bill. Is this the young man you were telling me about?"

"This is Allen. He's going to be staying with us for awhile. Allen, this is Skip Petersen. He has forgotten more about horses than I'll ever know," said Mr. Warner.

"Hi," answered Allen quietly.

"Why don't you head to town and run your errands, Bill. Allen and I can get to know each other a little bit and he can try a riding lesson with Angie if he wants," offered Skip.

"Is that okay with you, Allen?" asked Mr. Warner.

"Sure. Fine," answered Allen.

Skip gave Allen a tour of the big barn. It was L-shaped, with big box stalls on both sides of the aisle. Most of the stalls proudly displayed the horse's name and its owner. "How many horses do you have here?" asked Allen.

"Oh, anywhere from 40-50 at one time," answered Skip. "Most of them belong to boarders. I only have three horses of my own, these days. It's a lot of work, but I wouldn't want to do anything else."

They stopped in front of a stall with a big gray horse looking out. On the stall door it said "Finneus" in big letters.

"Thought you might like to meet him first. This is one of our best lesson horses. He's real patient with folks just starting out," said Skip. "Why don't you visit with him for a minute? I'll go look for Angie."

Allen was left alone with Finneus. The horse looked really big. A lot bigger than Ajax, the horse at Warner's farm. Finneus looked at Allen with his big gentle eyes and started looking for a treat.

"You don't get a treat until after the lesson, big guy," called a woman's voice. "Hi. I'm Angie. Skip said you might want a lesson."

"I'm not sure," answered Allen. "I haven't decided yet."

"That's fine," said Angie. "Why don't I show you how to brush him first. You can make up your mind about riding later."

Angie returned with a small box filled with grooming supplies. She snapped a lead rope on Finneus' halter and led him to the hitching rail.

Angie demonstrated. "First, we begin with a curry comb, like this. He loves it. In fact, sometimes he falls asleep."

It took almost 30 minutes, but when they were through, Finneus had been brushed until he shined.

"He's ready for a saddle now," said Angie. "Would you like to give it a try?"

"I guess so," answered Allen. "I'll try one lesson. But no promises about next week."

Allen felt tall aboard Finneus. The big gelding took slow gentle steps, as if he knew Allen was a first-time rider. By the end of the lesson, Allen was smiling a little.

"Great first time, Allen," called Angie. "Are you sure you've never ridden before?"

"No, I'm just a city kid," said Allen. "But I guess if I have to be with the Warners for awhile, I might as well give this a try."

"Great," answered Angie. "Same time next week then. Let's unsaddle Finneus and give him that treat he was looking for."

Allen continued weekly lessons with Angie for a month. After his lessons, he liked to wander through the barn and look at the other horses. One day he saw a new horse standing head-down in its stall. It was a chocolate brown Appaloosa with a white blanket. There was no name on the stall. "Where did that horse come from?" Allen asked Skip.

"That's Barney. He's just here for a few months. His owner had to move to another state and can't take care of him anymore."

"Is he for sale?" asked Allen.

"Oh, I guess not," answered Skip. "Barney's pretty old for a horse. Most people are looking for a younger horse."

"Well, how old does a horse get?" asked Allen.

"Finneus is 24. The oldest horse I ever had lived to be 35 years old. But older horses need special care and can't do the same kind of work as a young horse."

"Is Barney sick? He's just standing around, not even touching his hay," said Allen.

"No. I think he's depressed. I'll bet he just misses his owner. He's in a new place and doesn't have any friends," replied Skip.

"Can I be his friend?" asked Allen. "I can brush him and take him out of his stall to meet some of the other horses."

"I guess that would be fine," said Skip.

After each of his Saturday lessons, Allen made a habit of brushing Barney and taking him for walks around Twin Pines. Allen liked to sit in the grass and just watch Barney chomp grass and swish his tail. Barney was a good listener and Allen was happiest when he could spend time with the big gelding.

One day Allen was surprised to see Angie riding Barney when he and Mr. Warner pulled up for their lesson.

"That's Barney," Allen told Mr. Warner. "I've been helping Skip take care of him."

Angie waved. "How would you like to try a lesson on Barney today?"

"Really? Would it be okay?" asked Allen.

"He's feeling pretty good with all the extra

attention he's been getting from you. I think Barney's ready for some light riding," said Angie.

Mr. Warner stayed and watched Allen and Barney's lesson. With Allen on his back, Barney carried his tail a little higher and trotted with energy.

"Boy, you'd think he knew that he belonged to you," said Angie at the end of the lesson.

"What?" said Allen.

"Skip talked to Barney's owner last week. Barney's yours. That is, if you want him. He is pretty old, you know," said Mr. Warner.

"He's not that old," answered Allen. "Do you mean it? Could he really be mine?"

"We can bring him home to our barn this afternoon," said Mr. Warner. "But first I want to get some pictures of you and Barney. I know your grandma will want to see them when we visit her next week."

Allen grinned from ear to ear as he posed with his new best friend.

Rocking Horse Press

# Order Form

Name: Phone: ( )

Address: Fax #: ( )

City: State/Prov.:

Country: Postal Code/Zip:

E-Mail Address:

| Quantity | Item | Amount | Total |
|---|---|---|---|
| | The Power of Horses | $14.95 | |
| | The Magic of Horses | 14.95 | |
| | Forelocks, Fetlocks, and Horse Tales | 5.95 | |
| | Heart, Hoof & Soul | 7.95 | |
| Michigan Residents Add Sales Tax | | 6% | |
| Shipping (per item) | | 15% of order | |
| All Sales in U.S. Dollars | | Total Due | |

Payment by: ☐ Check ☐ Money Order

P.O. Box 21
Oshtemo, MI 49077-0021
Phone (269) 345-3783
E-Mail: info@rockinghorsepress.com
Web: www.rockinghorsepress.com